THE GENEVA
CHRONICLES

© 2022 BERGLI BOOKS, an imprint of HELVETIQ

All rights reserved.

www.bergli.ch

THE GENEVA CHRONICLES
AN ILLUSTRATED HISTORY AS TOLD BY ALLO THE ALLOBROGES AND HIS HORSE

ANITA LEHMANN

ILLUSTRATED BY
PIERRE WAZEM

To Robin, Hanna and Luca, and to all the brave explorers building a new life elsewhere **– AL**

TABLE OF CONTENTS

WELCOME TO GENEVA, BRAVE EXPLORER! 11

THE BEGINNINGS 15
HOW GARGANTUA CREATED LAKE GENEVA 16

ROMAN TIMES 19
CAESAR TAKES ON THE HELVETIANS 20

A TSUNAMI IN GENEVA 25
THE TAUREDUNUM EVENT 26

LATE MEDIEVAL TIMES 29
HOW THE MAISON TAVEL SURVIVED 32
10 FUNNY FACES: A MYSTERY 35

THE REFORMATION 37
HOW CALVIN BECAME GENEVAN 38
JEWELS AND WATCHES 46

THE ESCALADE 49

18TH CENTURY: A CENTURY OF IDEAS — 55
- LOCKED OUT: ROUSSEAU — 56
- DRAMA IN GENEVA: VOLTAIRE — 60
- MADAME DE STAËL ROCKS EUROPE — 64

19TH–21ST CENTURIES: GENEVA OPENS UP
- GENEVA BECOMES SWISS — 69
- BASHING THE BASTIONS — 70
- FRANKENSTEIN — 72
- THE JET D'EAU — 74
- HENRY DUNANT DREAMS BIG — 76
- A PALACE FOR PEACE – AND PEACOCKS — 78
- A CHAIR TO REMIND US — 82
- CERN: A WORLD-WIDE WEB OF SCIENCE — 84

GOODBYE! — 87

ILLUSTRATED TIMELINE — 88

ACKNOWLEDGEMENTS — 92

ABOUT THE AUTHOR AND ILLUSTRATOR — 95

WELCOME TO GENEVA, BRAVE EXPLORER!

> The word "Allobroges" is originally Celtic and means "The People from Elsewhere".

Welcome to Geneva, brave explorer!

I've been dead for over 2000 years, but you can still come and see my skeleton. It's buried deep underneath Geneva Cathedral, in the very heart of the city.

My people were called the Allobroges.

The People from Elsewhere . . . Like so many Genevans, we were strangers here at first. We came from somewhere else. But like many after us, we settled and stayed.

Did your family come from somewhere else, too?

I was the chieftain of my people.

When I died, people came to pray at my tomb. Later they built a memorial on top of it. Then, when Geneva became Christian, a church was built next to my memorial. Over the centuries, the church grew and changed, until today an entire cathedral is sitting on my bones. Fancy that!

I have witnessed everything that has happened as Geneva has grown and changed. I've seen dukes and duchesses, emperors and revolutionaries, warriors and writers come and go, armies march in and out. I've had my bones rattled by history.

And even though we Celts didn't know how to read or write, I do know how to tell a good tale.

So: Welcome to Geneva, brave explorer!

Let me tell you some stories from Geneva's history.

THE BEGINNINGS

ca. 20,000 BCE
A long, long time ago, tens of thousands of years before even we Allobroges settled here, legend says that a giant called Gargantua shaped the landscape around Geneva.

HOW GARGANTUA CREATED LAKE GENEVA

One steaming hot summer's day, the giant Gargantua was tramping about the area where Geneva is today. He was tired, sweaty, and desperately in need of a drink. He looked around for water, but all he could see was the river Rhone.

Now you might think the Rhone is a big river. But to this giant, it was no more than a tiny trickle.

Gargantua's hands were too large to scoop up any water. Luckily, he was a smart and inventive giant. With his left hand, he dug out the soil around the river. The river spilled into the hole he had made. This is how Gargantua created Lake Geneva.

Then, with his right hand, he built a mountain next to the lake using the soil he had scraped out of the hole. The people who lived in the area exclaimed:

"Ça lève!"

This is French for "It's rising!"

This is how Gargantua quenched his thirst, how Lake Geneva was formed, and how the mountain next to Geneva came to be called Salève.

In actual fact, Lake Geneva was formed about 20,000 years ago by a glacier flowing down from the Alps. Even today, you can still see two boulders that the glacier left behind. They sit in the lake, near the Jet d'Eau, and they are called the *Pierres du Niton* – the Niton Stones. These stones are used to measure the water level of the lake and are also a reference point for elevation measurements all around Switzerland.

ROMAN TIMES

Beginning around 121 BCE

CAESAR TAKES ON THE HELVETIANS

A long time ago, a tribe called the Helvetians lived in the area that is German-speaking Switzerland today. And if you believe the famous Roman emperor Julius Caesar, they were a crude and rowdy bunch.

In 58 BCE the Helvetians weren't happy with the land they lived on. They thought they could have a much better life elsewhere, and so they decided to move westwards, all the way towards the Atlantic Ocean. So they packed all their belongings, and to make sure that they wouldn't come back, they burned their huts and destroyed their fields. Then they walked westwards, towards . . . Geneva.

368,000 Helvetians! That's two thirds of the population of Geneva today — and hundreds of times the population of Geneva back in Roman times.

When the Helvetians reached Geneva, they knocked at the gates and asked for safe passage to cross the little bridge over the Rhone, pass through Geneva, and get to the land on the other side. They promised not to destroy anything, or to kill anyone, and generally to behave themselves.

The trouble was . . . there were 368,000 of them. And that's a lot of people!

The Genevans, who had been part of the Roman Empire since 121 BCE, imagined all those Helvetians trudging through their city, clogging up the roads and stealing food, horses and cattle. And they didn't want any of it. They were scared. So they called on the Roman commander-in-chief, who was none other than Julius Caesar, to come and sort things out for them.

Caesar disliked the Helvetians. Only a few years before, they had humiliated Rome by killing one of Caesar's colleagues and enslaving many Roman citizens. Caesar certainly wasn't going to help them now.

So as soon as he heard about the Helvetians, he gathered his troops and marched to Geneva.

He had a plan.

First, he dismantled the wooden bridge across the Rhone so no one could cross it.

Then he spoke to the Helvetian chieftains. He said that he had to think about their request to pass through Geneva, and they would just have to wait while he thought about it.

So the Helvetians waited. For two whole weeks.

During that time, Caesar's 6000 soldiers built a wall. Not just a garden wall, but a 14-kilometre-long fortification that led from the lake, along the Rhone, and all the way to the Jura mountains.

In this way, Caesar blocked the Helvetians from being able to pass anywhere near Geneva.

"NON POSSUMUS" is Latin and means "we can't". What Caesar meant was "We can't let you pass (sorry not sorry at all)."

Only then did he turn to the Helvetians, who were still waiting patiently. He shrugged his shoulders, smiled a sly smile, and said, *"Non possumus."*

The Helvetians were furious. They were hungry and tired and desperate to move on. Some jumped into the Rhone and tried to swim across, but the Genevans stopped them from reaching the other bank. Others tried to cross further down the Rhone, but they bumped into Caesar's wall. Caesar had tricked them. Their way was blocked.

So the Helvetians had to turn around and keep on trudging, knowing that the path they would have to take would be much longer and more difficult. In the end, they failed. They had no choice but to return to their former home, to their burnt-out houses and their ruined fields.

And Caesar patted himself on the shoulder, and wrote the whole story down.

A TSUNAMI IN GENEVA

Around 563 CE

THE TAUREDUNUM EVENT

In 563 CE, a whole mountainside collapsed near Tauredunum at the eastern end of Lake Geneva.

This huge landslide caused the lake waters to swell without warning. A tsunami – a gigantic wave – raced across the lake. By the time the wave had reached Geneva it was 8 metres high! It destroyed boats, mills and bridges, and flooded everything on the lakeshore. Then it smashed into and surged over Geneva's city walls. I can tell you, my bones rattled from the impact!

LATE MEDIEVAL TIMES

13th to 15th centuries

In late medieval times, merchants from all over Europe gathered in Geneva to trade horses, pigs and chickens; cloth from France and Belgium; furs from the north; silk from Italy; and gold and spices from Africa and Asia.

It was a time of great fairs, which were like huge parties that lasted for weeks. I still remember the smells of incense, cinnamon and expensive perfume – but also of sweaty people, pigs' pee and horse poo.

These fairs made Geneva famous, and it became a large and lively medieval city. One house in Geneva was particularly important: the Maison Tavel. Its cellars were used for trading and for storing cloth, spices and other merchandise.

HOW THE MAISON TAVEL SURVIVED

In the 17th and 18th centuries, many medieval houses in Geneva were destroyed to make room for more more modern ones. The owners of the Maison Tavel might have thought about doing the same. However, while digging in their garden one day, they discovered some Roman coins, along with broken pieces of pots and plates that were more than a thousand years old. It was a sure sign that people had lived there in Roman times.

After this, a rumour sprang up and spread like wildfire through the streets of Geneva, giving the Maison Tavel an air of mystery and awe. It was whispered that many, many years ago, the great Roman Emperor Julius Caesar had slept there!

Today, the Maison Tavel is a museum. When you next go there, try to find a little room among the cellars, all the way at the back. This was the safe where the Tavel family would have stored all their important papers and family archives (and maybe even some treasure...)

The owners of the house might have liked the idea that they were connected to the famous Julius Caesar. Perhaps this is why the Maison Tavel still stands today, while most other medieval buildings in Geneva have been demolished.

10 FUNNY FACES: A MYSTERY

These ten faces have looked out from the Maison Tavel for nearly 800 years.

The artists who made them used codes – like a secret language – to tell their story. Sadly, the key to this secret language has been lost, and not even the cleverest historian can be sure of what the faces are really trying to say.

What do you think they are telling us?

THE REFORMATION
16th century

The time of the Reformation was a time of open and very nasty warfare between Catholics and Protestants in Europe: Catholics hunted down Protestants, and Protestants hunted down Catholics. People on both sides were beheaded, burned, or hanged for their faith. The war between Protestants and Catholics lasted for over a hundred years and many people had to flee their country.

HOW CALVIN BECAME GENEVAN

John Calvin was a refugee. He had to escape his home country, France, because the king of France, a Catholic, was chasing down and killing Protestants – and Calvin was a Protestant. He wanted to reform the church, to make it better. He arrived in Geneva with a bundle of clothes, a Bible, and some very strong beliefs.

In Geneva, the fiery preacher Guillaume Farel had sparked the Reformation, but he wasn't very popular. He needed a convincing preacher to help truly bring the Reformation to the city. So Calvin and Farel paired up to reform Geneva – and its people!

Calvin's Academy later became the University of Geneva!

Before the 16th century, the streets of Geneva were a smelly mess! People didn't have toilets at home, so they would do their business on a chamber pot, and then throw the contents straight onto the road outside their window.

SOME PEOPLE THOUGHT that Calvin was simply the best thing that had ever happened to Geneva.

Before the Reformation, very few children went to school, and only the very rich knew how to read and write. Calvin wanted to change that. He wanted everybody to be able to read, and especially to be able to read the Bible. So not only did he help translate the Bible from Latin into French – he also created a whole new school system in which all children, rich and poor, could learn to read and write.

Not only that – Calvin also set up the Academy, a school for adults. Students could come to Geneva, learn all about the Christian faith Calvin-style, and then go back to their country to share Calvin's Reformation with the rest of the world.

Calvin also worked to make the city a clean and safe place for everyone. For example, he installed a new drainage system, which meant that Geneva became a much nicer (and less smelly) place to live.

OTHERS THOUGHT that Calvin was simply the worst thing that had ever happened to Geneva.

Calvin was sure that his beliefs were the right ones. He was so sure about them that he would fly into a rage whenever anyone disagreed with him. But the problem wasn't just his temper – it was also that his faith was very, very strict. He led a simple, hard-working and quiet life, and he thought that all Genevans should be just like him. Everyone else should also live a simple, hard-working and quiet life. With the help of the Consistory, a church council that he was in charge of, Calvin set about changing how everyone behaved. He was going to make Geneva into a model city of the Reformation, whether the people of Geneva wanted it or not!

The Consistory condemned and punished anything it saw as luxury. For example, dancing, parties, fancy jewellery, gambling, and even women curling their hair were all FORBIDDEN!

Some of these laws had been there before, but the Genevans had never taken them seriously. Now everyone, from the poorest beggar to the richest man in town, had to stick to the rules. On top of that,

the Consistory had spies all over Geneva. These spies would watch and listen to what people did and said at work, at school, and even at home.

Two true stories:
A man named Pierre enjoyed just ambling about town, his fingers full of rings and his chest covered in gold chains.

But . . .

Pierre was told off for being too fanciful. (We don't know what happened to his jewellery.)

A woman named Francesca wanted to enjoy herself, and danced at her own wedding.

But . . .

Francesca was thrown into prison as a punishment for DANCING! (But not without putting up a good fight. "Pig! Liar! Swineherd!" she shouted as she was being dragged away.)

Calvin was resented not only for the things he said, but also because he was a foreigner. The old Genevan families feared that he was having a dangerous influence on their city.

These families had held power in the city for generations, and now along came this French know-it-all telling them what to do, what to wear and how to behave!

For many years, wherever Calvin walked, people hurled insults at him. Some even named their dogs after him.

Calvin always wore gloves because he was worried that someone might try to poison him through the skin of his hands. That may seem crazy, but it really was true that people wanted to get rid of him. One winter day a stranger leapt out of the darkness and tried to push him off an icy bridge and into the Rhone.

Despite these threats, Calvin never stopped working. Every single day, he put on his black robes and went out to preach. Even when he was spat at on the streets, even when he was sick and coughing (which was a lot!),

even when his wife was dying, he went out to preach because he believed that that was what he had to do.

Because of Calvin's relentless work, Geneva became famous as a stronghold of the Reformation, a safe place for Protestant refugees to go. Many of these refugees were specialists in watchmaking, cloth-making and printing. As the refugees flowed in, the population of the city doubled – from 10,000 to 20,000 inhabitants in only ten years. Geneva, closed in behind its thick walls, suddenly felt very small.

With the refugees' arrival, Calvin's influence grew – and the old Genevan families' power faded. Over the years, the people of Geneva began to believe what Calvin taught. They began to respect him. By 1555, most of Calvin's enemies had left Geneva for good. Some had had their heads chopped off. Others had been banished. And others simply came to accept the Frenchman and his strict new ways. The Protestant refugees gained influence in the city. They started running the place. And this is how, in the 16th century, Calvin and his fellow refugees became the new Genevans.

Guillaume Farel (1489–1565) *Fiery Farel: He sparked the Reformation in Geneva.*
John Calvin (1509–1564): *He coughed a lot, but he sure reformed the city.*
Théodore de Bèze (1519–1605): *He took over Geneva's church when Calvin died, and is said to have snored all the way through the battle of the Escalade! (But, to be fair, by the time of the Escalade he was very, very old – and deaf.)*
John Knox (1513–1572): *A huge fan of Calvin who lived in Geneva for three years. He brought the Reformation from Geneva all the way to Scotland and made life hell for Mary Queen of Scots. All in the name of religion, of course.*

JEWELS AND WATCHES

Calvin and his fellow reformers forbade jewellery. They hated luxury, and felt that pieces of jewellery such as necklaces, bracelets and earrings were useless extravagances that nobody should possess.

The Genevan jewellery makers became desperate: How could they earn their living? How would they feed their families if they were no longer allowed to make and sell their jewellery?

Luckily for the jewellers, the reformers didn't see watches as a useless indulgence. Watches were very useful, in fact. So the Genevan jewellers stopped making jewellery and learned how to make watches instead.

Elisabeth Baulacre (1613–1693) was the daughter of protestant refugees. From running a small haberdashery, she worked her way up to a gold thread emporium with business all over Europe. By the time she died, she had become part of Geneva's jetset – the second richest person in town!

Even more luckily, the Protestant refugees brought with them many new skills – including watchmaking – so the local jewellers were able to learn from them. Soon, Geneva's ex-jewellers and Geneva's skilful refugees were busy making watches in all kinds of shapes and sizes: flowery watches, animal watches, fruit watches, watches to hang around your neck (pendant watches), and clockwork automatons.

This is how Genevans became famous as watchmakers.

THE ESCALADE

1602

One freezing December night in 1602, the people of Geneva were snuggled up in their beds, unaware that there might be danger lurking outside the city gates. But outside the walls, on the Plaine de Plainpalais, the fields were filling up with Savoyard soldiers!

The Duke of Savoy had come to try to conquer this rich and beautiful city. He wanted to make it Catholic once again. And he wanted to do this even though, just a few weeks earlier, he had signed a treaty promising not to attack Geneva.

The Savoyard horses had cloth tied around their hooves so that nobody could hear them. The soldiers had smeared their faces with charcoal so that nobody could see them. Some of them carried long wooden ladders. These soldiers were going to climb the city walls, sneak through the quiet streets, open the gates, and let the rest of the army into the city.

Just as the first Savoyards climbed over the wall into the city, two Genevan guards came upon them. One of the guards was killed on the spot, but the other managed to raise the alarm. At 2:30 a.m. the cathedral bells started ringing.

And thus began the battle of the Escalade.

The bells rang loudly – so loudly that my bones rattled down in the cellar of the cathedral. And the Genevans jumped out of their beds.

Still in their nightshirts, they grabbed swords, chairs, sticks, rocks, and whatever else they could get hold of, and went off to fight the invaders.

> "L'Escalade" means "climbing" in French.

> "A sneaky surprise attack! What cheek, what a disgrace for the people of Savoy! In Allobrogian times, a man like that sleazy Duke would have had his head cut off and stuck on a large pole by the city gates to serve as a warning to others!"

THE MYTH OF MÈRE ROYAUME (MOTHER KINGDOM)

That very night, it is said, a woman named Catherine Royaume happened to be making vegetable soup for her fourteen children. It was bubbling away in a cauldron on the stove.

When Catherine heard the alarm, she grabbed the big bubbling cauldron and carried it across to her kitchen window. She tipped the boiling hot contents over the Savoyards on their ladders below – carrots, leeks, celery and all!

This is how Catherine Royaume became the famous Mère Royaume (Mother Kingdom).

The Duke of Savoy had to withdraw his troops and admit defeat. He also had to sign another peace treaty. And this time he stuck to it.

Every year, on the day of the Escalade, the people of Geneva celebrate their victory. They buy or make chocolate cauldrons (*marmite* in French) and fill them with marzipan vegetables to remember Mère Royaume and her soup. The soup that saved their city!

18TH CENTURY
A CENTURY OF IDEAS

The 18th century is also called the "Century of Ideas". This is because people all over Europe started asking lots of questions about the world they lived in. They thought about the roles of kings and queens and wondered whether the world would be a better place if there were no kings and queens at all, and ordinary people had more power. Into that century were born some of Geneva's most famous inhabitants: Jean-Jacques Rousseau, Voltaire, and Germaine de Staël.

LOCKED OUT: ROUSSEAU

Jean-Jacques Rousseau (1712–1778) was a dreamer. When he was an awkward teenager, he loved reading and thinking and wandering about the countryside. He was supposed to be learning to be an engraver with a man called Master Ducommun in Geneva's old town. (At that time, an engraver in Geneva would mostly have decorated watches.) But while Jean-Jacques enjoyed engraving, he wasn't the speediest apprentice. On the contrary, he was very, very slow.

Master Ducommun didn't want a dreamy apprentice! He wanted an apprentice who worked hard and fast, so he often scolded and beat Jean-Jacques.

To get away from all the scolding and beating, Jean-Jacques escaped to the fields and woods around Geneva whenever he could. He often came back only at nightfall, just before the city gates closed for the night.

One Sunday afternoon, Jean-Jacques was out late. From far away, he heard the drums announcing the closing of the city gates. He ran toward them, but he was too far away. He sprinted as fast as he could, shouting to the guards to hold on, to wait . . .

But it was too late.

The drawbridge slowly rose up into the air. Jean-Jacques threw himself onto the ground, pleading with the soldiers to lower it again for him. But the guards only shook their heads.

Jean-Jacques Rousseau found himself locked out of Geneva. So he picked himself up, shook the dust out of his clothes, and looked hard at the city walls. That was the moment he decided to leave Geneva. He turned and walked off into the dusk to explore the big world beyond Geneva's walls.

For the rest of his life, Jean-Jacques Rousseau travelled around France, Switzerland and England. He read a lot, he studied, and he wrote a great many books himself.

He became one of Europe's most famous and feared writers and philosophers.

He wrote things such as "Man is born free, and yet he is everywhere in chains!"

Rousseau's books "Emile" and "The Social Contract" were burned in front of Geneva's town hall, because they directly attacked the way Genevan society worked.

Rousseau's ideas were bold and revolutionary. His books spoke of freedom and democracy. He got into serious trouble for them, because they directly attacked the rich and powerful everywhere. He was kicked out of France, had to sneak away from Geneva, and was declared undesirable in Bern. Wherever he went, people sent him away. His pen was too dangerous, so nobody wanted him around.

But while kings, queens and other powerful people everywhere hated and feared Rousseau, the people loved his ideas.

Rousseau died in 1778, so he never saw the great changes his ideas helped set off. Eleven years after his death, the French Revolution erupted in Paris. The King was toppled. People hoped to build a democracy – a country where the people ruled. Rousseau became a hero of the French Revolution, and, later, a hero of other revolutions all around the world.

Revolution also hit Geneva. In an uprising in 1792, the people ousted the ruling families, and formed a new government.

In 1798, Emperor Napoleon marched in, occupied Geneva, and spoiled it all for the Genevan revolution. When he finally left in 1815, the old order came back in full force. This is known as the Restoration — but that's another story altogether!

Fifty years after his death, the people of Geneva claimed Rousseau back. They collected money to build a statue in his honour. When it was ready, on 24 February 1835, people queued up along the quays of Geneva to the sounds of rolling drums and blaring trumpets, craning their necks to get a glimpse of the brand-new statue appearing from under a green cloth on the freshly re-named *Île Rousseau*.

If Master Ducommun hadn't been quite so harsh with Rousseau, he might have stayed in Geneva and become one of its many watch engravers. He might never have shaken the world with his ideas.

Fancy that!

DRAMA IN GENEVA: VOLTAIRE

Voltaire (1694–1778) lived in Geneva from 1755 to 1765.

He was smart and witty – and didn't he know it!

Kings and queens all over Europe admired Voltaire and his writing. But they couldn't bear to have him near them for too long, because they were afraid of his sharp tongue.

Voltaire wasn't allowed to live in Paris because he had poked fun at the French king. When he also fell out with King Frederick of Prussia, he moved to a country house just outside of Geneva, together with a few cows, an eagle, and a monkey named Luc.

Voltaire called his house *Les Délices* – "the Delights".

He had six horses to pull his four carriages. He wore extravagant clothes and jewellery, and he decorated his house with the most exclusive, expensive furniture and pictures.

At that time, however, the very Calvinist Genevans were supposed to avoid luxury of any kind.

Voltaire also loved theatre and drama, but theatre was – you guessed it! – strictly forbidden as well.

> Luc was not only the monkey's name, it was also Voltaire's nickname for Frederick, King of Prussia. Luc the monkey sometimes bit Voltaire's ankle, but Voltaire kept him anyway.

> In 18th-century Geneva, showing off and luxury were strictly prohibited. For example, if people wanted to go somewhere in the city, they had to walk. Travelling in a horse-drawn carriage was forbidden, as it was seen as lazy.

Voltaire didn't pay much attention to Geneva's laws. He staged his own plays in his own house. He even had a theatre built at Les Délices. When it was ready, he invited all of the important Genevan families to come watch his play *Zaïre*.

The Genevans were fascinated by the flamboyant Voltaire. So even though they felt uncomfortable, they came to see the play.

Les Délices soon became the most fashionable place to visit near Geneva. But Voltaire kept getting into trouble.

Geneva's laws said that he had too many horses, too many carriages, too many decorations, too much luxury, and, worst of all . . . too much drama at his house.

Voltaire clearly had to find somewhere else to live.

So he bought a castle in the village of Ferney – just outside of Geneva, but in France. There he could do as he liked. Many years later, Ferney even changed its name to honour him. It is now called Ferney-Voltaire.

MADAME DE STAËL ROCKS EUROPE

In 1799 Napoleon Bonaparte became the ruler of France.

Germaine de Staël (1766–1817), the daughter of the Genevan banker Jacques Necker, hoped that Napoleon would be a wise leader, and that he would bring peace and democracy to France.

But Napoleon turned out to be a tyrant, ever greedier for power and fame. He wasn't interested in democracy and peace. He was interested in ruling an empire: not just France, but all of Europe.

Living in Paris, Madame de Staël saw that Napoleon was dangerously hungry for power, so she decided to work against him. At that time, however, women weren't allowed to participate in politics. So if she wanted to change the world, she was going to have to get powerful men to listen to her.

Luckily, Madame de Staël knew how to make people listen to her. It was, in fact, her speciality! She always carried a willow twig, and twirled it in her fingers whilst talking to people, just like a conductor wielding a baton.

At her "salons" Madame de Staël brought together kings and queens and the most famous politicians, philosophers and artists of her time. They would all gather to discuss what was happening in the world.

And in front of all these important people, Madame de Staël criticised Napoleon.

That got up Napoleon's nose! He got so scared of Madame de Staël's influence that he banned her from Paris. So she moved to her father's castle in Coppet, near Geneva. She missed her busy life and her friends from Paris, and felt very lonely, but she kept holding her salons. She wrote letters and books.

She travelled around Europe, twirling her willow twig, making people listen to her, negotiating and discussing.

One of the books Madame de Staël wrote was called *Germany*. It was about German culture and politics, and was very critical of what was happening in France. Napoleon forbade its publication, and Madame de Staël was furious. She was going to get her book published, no matter what! But by now she was under house arrest and wasn't allowed to travel any further than Geneva. Napoleon even had spies in her household. The spies watched and reported on her every move.

Madame de Staël wasn't having any of this. In 1812, she stepped into a horse-drawn carriage outside her castle in Coppet, carrying only her fan, pretending that she was going for a little tour around the village. In reality, she set out on a secret trip across Europe.

> Not only did he have to abdicate, but he was also banished to the tiny island of St Helena, way out in the Atlantic Ocean, where the only thing he could fight were coconuts.

She had to be very careful. Europe was at war, and the trip was dangerous – Napoleon's spies and armies were everywhere. She travelled to Vienna first, and then via Russia and Sweden all the way to England.

It took Madame de Staël a whole year to get from Coppet to London, where *Germany* was finally published. But she did it. Germaine de Staël: 1. Napoleon: 0.

Napoleon lost the war that he had started in Europe. In 1815, his power collapsed completely.

Madame de Staël kept writing and holding salons, wielding her willow stick, and working for the ideas she believed in. So great was this Genevan woman's influence that in 1815 it was said that there were only three powers that really counted in Europe:

France, England, and Germaine de Staël!

19ᵀᴴ–21ˢᵀ CENTURIES
GENEVA OPENS UP

GENEVA BECOMES SWISS

In 1815, Geneva joined Switzerland as the country's 22nd canton.

BASHING THE BASTIONS

Auguste Magnin (1841–1903) loved Geneva, and he particularly liked the city walls: the bastions. There were a lot of bastions in Geneva because for hundreds of years it had been an independent city-state, and people had built wall after wall to protect themselves. But now Geneva no longer needed all those walls. It wasn't under attack anymore. It had become a part of Switzerland – and what was more, the city was growing. To many Genevans, the bastions were old-fashioned and unnecessary. They wanted Geneva to become larger and grander – and the bastions stood in the way. So starting in 1850, the bastions were ripped down. They made way for things like airy boulevards, Geneva's first proper theatre (the Grand-Théâtre), the railway station, and the Parc des Bastions.

Auguste Magnin was devastated at losing the bastions, and very sad that his beloved city was changing forever. He was an architect, and he set about building a small model of the Geneva he had known. He spent many years absorbed in the task, paying attention to the smallest details, in order to preserve the Geneva of his childhood for generations to come. Today, you can still admire his work, the Magnin Relief, on the top floor of the Maison Tavel.

FRANKENSTEIN

During the 19th century the first English tourists arrived in Geneva. They came for the fresh air, the spring water, and to admire Switzerland's lakes and mountains. Among these tourists was an eighteen-year-old English woman named Mary Godwin.

One stormy night in a house near Geneva, Mary Godwin and her friends decided to have a competition:

Who could write the scariest horror story of them all?

A few nights later, Mary dreamed about a scientist who discovered how to create a living being. He stuck bits and pieces of skin, muscle and bone together, formed them into a man, and brought the man to life. The scientist, whose name was Dr Frankenstein, had hoped to make a beautiful man – but instead he created a hideous monster!

Mary took her dream as an inspiration, sat down, and wrote her novel *Frankenstein*, which became world famous. Some say that it is the first science fiction novel ever written.

You can find a statue of Frankenstein's monster on the Plaine de Plainpalais.

THE JET D'EAU

JET D'EAU FACTS
Height: 140 metres (as high as 20 houses) — one of the ten highest fountains in the world!
Speed of the water: 200 km/hour (almost twice as fast as a car zooming along the motorway).

In the 19th century many watchmakers had their workshops along the river Rhone. They used the flow of the water to help power their machines. In the evening, when the workmen stopped using their machines for the night, the water from the river would continue flowing into the system, creating too much pressure. To relieve that pressure, engineers created a safety valve, a hole through which the excess water could escape when the pressure got too high. This is how the Jet d'Eau was born.

The Jet d'Eau was not only practical – it was also pretty. People kept visiting it to see the water shoot up, and it became a tourist attraction. In 1891, a newer and larger version of the Jet d'Eau was built on the lake, and in 1951 an extra-strong pumping system was installed, making the water spout up even higher.

HENRY DUNANT DREAMS BIG

Henry Dunant (1828–1910) liked to dream big. He dreamed about becoming a successful businessman and mingling with the rich and powerful of Geneva. He also dreamed about helping people in need and making the world a better place.

In 1859 he tried to get the emperor of France to help him with his business. The emperor, however, was busy fighting a war in Italy. Dunant followed him. He arrived in the town of Solferino a few hours after a huge battle had raged.

Henry Dunant saw soldiers lying in pools of blood, wounded, dead and dying. He saw men bleeding from wounds that could have been patched up, men begging for a drink and pleading for help.

300,000 soldiers fought in the battle of Solferino. 23,000 of them were killed or wounded.

But there weren't enough people to help!

That day, Henry Dunant rallied the people of Solferino. Together, they did what they could for the soldiers. They dressed wounds. They brought water to those who needed it. They comforted the soldiers who were dying.

Back home in Geneva, Henry Dunant couldn't stop thinking about what he had seen. He wrote and published a book called *A Memory of Solferino*. In it, he argues that if a soldier risks his life at war, someone should look after him if he gets wounded, no matter which side the soldier is fighting for.

Henry Dunant received letters of praise and support not only from ordinary people, but also from kings and queens, princes and generals, all over Europe. They liked Henry Dunant's ideas. Some wanted to help turn them into reality.

With their support, Henry Dunant founded a new organisation in Geneva, an organisation which would later be called the ICRC: the International Committee of the Red Cross.

However, Henry Dunant's dreams of becoming a successful businessman failed. He had asked many of his friends and family to lend him money for his business. The business collapsed, leaving him with a mountain of debt. His family and friends were upset that they had lost their money, and they turned against him.

Henry Dunant had to resign from the Red Cross. He escaped from Geneva at night and travelled across Europe as a poor man. He never came back to his hometown. For a while he was homeless and had to sleep on park benches.

Then, in 1901, a journalist found out about Henry Dunant's story and wrote about it. People read the story and came to appreciate what he had done many years before. So it happened that, at the end of his life, Henry Dunant finally got recognised for his work in founding the Red Cross. He was awarded the first-ever Nobel Peace Prize.

Today, you can find a bust of Henry Dunant on the Place de Neuve. His bust sits right where the gallows used to be!

A PALACE FOR PEACE – AND PEACOCKS

Gustave Revilliod (1817–1890) was an art collector. He also loved nature, travelling – and peacocks. Wherever he travelled, he would collect pictures, objects, and samples of trees – sequoias from California, eucalyptus from Asia, cedars from Lebanon. Luckily, he owned both a large house and a huge park, so there was space for all the things he brought back home, and for all the trees and birds. He called the park Ariana, after his mother. Here he planted the trees he brought home from all over the world. And here his peacocks roamed about freely.

When Revilliod died, he gave the park to the city of Geneva. He couldn't have dreamed that, many years later, the Ariana Park would not only be a place for trees and peacocks, but also for important people from all over the world.

How did this come about? From 1914 to 1918, a war shook Europe: the First World War. It killed millions of people, and when at last it was over, people had a single wish on their lips:

"NEVER AGAIN WAR!"

Because of this wish, 42 different countries came together to form an organisation to work towards peace:

The League of Nations.

The League of Nations chose Geneva to be its meeting place. It had huge hopes for peace, and so it needed a huge building. It couldn't just be a house, or even a hall. It had to be a Palace for Peace – A Palace of Nations.

To build a palace, they needed land. So the city of Geneva gave them part of Gustave Revilliod's Ariana Park to build on.

All the different member countries contributed something towards the building: stone, wood, and other building materials. The Italians provided marble for the floors and walls, the Belgians glass for the windows. Later, for another building, the Philippines provided coconut matting for the floors.

Into the very first stone of the building, they sealed a time capsule. It contains a letter in English and French explaining the ideas behind the League of Nations, and sample coins from all the member countries, so that, centuries later, people will still be able to understand what this building was all about... The Palace of Nations is huge! It's one of the ten largest buildings in Europe today.

The League of Nations wanted to end war, and to promote peace. Sadly, it failed in its mission. In 1939, the Second World War broke out. After the war, the League of Nations was replaced by a new but similar organisation: the United Nations.

The United Nations took over the Palace of Nations as a meeting place, a place to come together and find peaceful solutions to prevent wars.

Today, 193 countries are members of the United Nations. From the Place des Nations, you can see all of their flags waving in the wind.

And just as Gustave Revilliod would have wished, his trees are still looked after (there are over 800 different species now). And peacocks still roam freely in the Parc des Nations.

A CHAIR TO REMIND US

This gigantic broken chair was created in 1997 as part of a campaign to stop the use of landmines, and to encourage all countries to sign a treaty against them – the Mine Ban Treaty. A landmine is a type of bomb placed on or just under the surface of the ground. It explodes when someone steps on it. Sometimes, a landmine is placed during a war, but doesn't explode until many years later. People who step on a leftover landmine might die, or lose an arm or a leg in the explosion. That's why the chair has a broken-off leg.

CERN: A WORLD-WIDE WEB OF SCIENCE

In 1945, towards the end of the Second World War, two atomic bombs were dropped on the Japanese cities Hiroshima and Nagasaki. These weapons of mass destruction were a brand new invention. Nobody had ever used them before. The atomic bombs killed hundreds of thousands of people and injured many more.

One of the physicists who helped create those bombs was named Julius Robert Oppenheimer. He felt terrible about using his knowledge to make such awful weapons. After the war, he and some physicist friends wanted to make sure that science would help the world, not destroy it. They wanted physics to be used for peace.

CERN stands for "Conseil Européen pour Recherche Nucleaire" — European Council for Nuclear Research (or European Laboratory for Particle Physics). Today, 22 countries support CERN.

So they worked towards the creation of a new international organisation in Europe – a research organisation for nuclear physics. Thanks to their work, twelve European countries set up CERN in Geneva in 1952.

They chose Geneva because it had already hosted the League of Nations. Also, Geneva was in Switzerland, a neutral country. This was especially important right after the Second World War, because CERN had to be seen as neutral, as well.

The twelve countries shared the cost for the large, complex machines and equipment necessary for the research. They also agreed to share all of the discoveries made at CERN with the whole world. That way all the countries in the world would receive the same information at the same time, and nobody could take advantage of secret knowledge.

Today, scientists from all over the world come to work together at CERN to find out what makes the universe tick. They do this by studying particles. Particles are so tiny you can't see them, feel them, or hear them. They have funky names like quarks, leptons and gravitons. Even though they are small, particles are important because together they make up "matter". Matter, in turn, is everything you can see or touch.

By observing particles, scientists hope to find out what our universe is made of, and what might happen to it in the future. At CERN, the tiniest particles are helping us find answers to these enormous questions.

Fancy that!

GOODBYE!

I have told you a great many stories, About warriors like Caesar, brave women like Catherine Royaume, refugees like Calvin, nomads like Rousseau, fighters like Madame de Staël, dreamers like Henry Dunant.

Fancy that, a little city like Geneva, with all these people coming and going!

So, welcome to Geneva, brave explorer!

Where do you come from? And where will you go from here, I wonder?

Pop by some time to catch up with my bones underneath the Cathedral. I'm sure I will be glad to see you.

10,000 BCE
First traces of people living in the Geneva area.

Ca. 200 BCE
Allobrogian times.

563 CE
Tauredunum Event: a tsunami in Geneva.

11th–14th century
The time of the great fairs. People from all over Europe flock to Geneva to trade their goods.

1558
John Calvin establishes the Academy, which will later become the University of Geneva.

1602
The Escalade: The Duke of Savoy tries to win Geneva back, but fails.

Ca. 121 BCE
Geneva is occupied by the Romans.

58 BCE
Caesar stops the Helvetians from passing through Geneva.
GENAVA: The first time the name "Genava" is written down (by Caesar).

1334
A fire destroys most of Geneva. The Maison Tavel burns down and is re-built. 10 funny faces are put on the façade.

1536
Geneva breaks free of Savoy rule and becomes an independent city state. In the same year, the city adopts the Reformation.

1755
Voltaire comes to live in Geneva, creating all sorts of mayhem and outrage.

1762
Jean-Jacques Rousseau's books *Emile* and *The Social Contract* are forbidden in Geneva, and are burned in front of the town hall.

1792
Revolution in Geneva.
The Genevan oligarchy is toppled,
and the people seize power.

1798–1813
Geneva occupied by France.

1872
Calvin's Academy becomes
the University of Geneva.

1891
The Jet d'Eau moves to the lake and
becomes a Genevan landmark.

1997
A giant chair with a missing leg is
placed on the Place des Nations – a
symbol of the campaign against land
mines and for human dignity.

2008
The Large Hadron Collider is built at CERN,
Geneva, where scientists hope to find
out about the secrets of the universe.

1815
Geneva becomes Swiss.

1863
Henry Dunant sets up the International Committee of the Red Cross in Geneva.

1919
The League of Nations chooses Geneva as its headquarters. Construction is begun on the Palace of Nations.

1945
The United Nations take over the Palace of Nations as its headquarters in Europe.

THANK YOU

This book took a long time to be born, and I would like to thank a great many people for helping me along the way:

Joy Manné and Laurie Theurer, my partners-in-writing who patiently read this text over and over (and over!) again.

Denise Nickerson for first putting money on its creation.

Agathe Chevalier for her leap of faith translating this book long before getting paid for it.

The S.H.A.G. (Société Historique et Archéologique de Genève) for giving valuable feedback on my research and writing, in particular Dr. Marc-André Haldimann (Allobroges and Romans) and Dr. Flavio Borda d'Agua (Musée Voltaire).

Dr. Alexandre Fiett (Maison Tavel), Dr. Isabelle Graessle (Reformation museum), Dr. Philip Benedict (Institut de la Réforme, Geneva), Rémy Hildebrand (Maison de Rousseau et de la Littérature), Gregory Meyer (International Geneva), artist Daniel Berset (broken chair), Kristine Greenaway (Germaine de Staël and Voltaire), François Briard (CERN), Jean-François Boquet (watch making) and Elizabeth Hornor Boquet (for her poetry, and for always making me laugh).

The Geneva Writers Group and SCBWI Switzerland for being brilliant at nurturing writers.

Joseph Hahnhart for believing in this project, and for introducing me to Pierre Wazem.

Séverine Jacomy-Vité for storing the 'Vin des Allobroges' in Salvan.

The team at Bergli Books, the Loterie Romande and the Fondation Henri Moser for helping to make it happen.

My parents who still love me even though I haven't become a diplomat. My sister, for her quiet, steady faith. My husband for his love and patience against all odds. And my children, for inspiring this book in the first place.

ANITA LEHMANN

PIERRE WAZEM

Born and bred in Bern, Switzerland, Anita Lehmann is an award-winning author with an MA in Social and Economic History from the University of Geneva. Passionate about local history as a tool for integration, she started writing **The Geneva Chronicles** in 2014 for her young son after the family's move to Geneva. This is her ninth book.

Recent titles:

Goodnight, Switzerland
(Helvetiq, Lausanne, 2021)
50 Amazing Swiss Women (co-author
(co-author) (Bergli Books, Basel, 2021)
The Princess and the Prick
(Harper Collins, London, 2020)

www.anita-lehmann.com

Born in 1970, Pierre published his first comic strips in **Sauve qui peut**. As both a comics scripter and comic book artist, his style ranges from cartoons to the realistic. He has worked both alone and in collaborations. He designs theatre sets and creates murals for both private individuals and institutions as well as staging "design concerts" and producing animation, children's illustrations, press cartoons, and exhibits all over the world. He has won numerous awards and teaches at the Ceruleum school of visual arts in Lausanne. His thirty or so comic books have been translated into a dozen languages. He does his work in Studios Lolos, Geneva.

Most recent publication:

En Coulisse
Edition Atrabile Genève

http://pierrewazem.tumblr.com

With generous support of:

& **FONDATION HENRI MOSER**

Bergli Books is being supported by the **Swiss Federal Office of Culture** with a structural grant for the years 2021–2025.

THE GENEVA CHRONICLES: AN ILLUSTRATED HISTORY AS TOLD BY ALLO THE ALLOBROGES AND HIS HORSE

Text: **Anita Lehmann**

Illustrations : **Pierre Wazem**

Design and typesetting : **Chloé Vargoz**

ISBN : 978-3-03869-094-8

1st edition: April 2022

All rights reserved.

Printed in the Czech Republic